WEALTH CREATION

THE TRUST

Trust is the greatest source that brings forth the best results. It's invaluable!

Rob Wilson

Dedication

These series of Wealth Creation is dedicated to the many families that I have comes across in my work. It is also dedicated to you the now reader, whether you are reading just this book or the entire series, I am in prayer that you experience wealth creation personally.

I especially wish that you who have chosen to read this series find what they are seeking.

To: *Pastor Allen*

[signature]

Rob Wilson   5/21/23

INVALUABLE

Focus require commitment, commitment is best done when you know your purpose. It's what inspires you while taking action.

Table of Contents

Foreword

As a Pastor and a therapist, I have learned that every relationship relies on and thrives in an atmosphere of trust.

That includes spouses in a marriage, co-workers on a job, employers with employees, neighbors in a community, teachers with students, mentors with mentees, law enforcement with the community, and even the President with the citizens of a country.

From a non-organic standpoint, there is a relationship that gets formed with money. There is a trust factor involved in that relationship as well. Our pastor (Bishop Dale C. Bronner) often says:

"You never have to choose between God and money. You just have to choose which one you will serve."

In other words, you ought to be the type of person who can be trusted with money because you know it is a resource. Not the source. Rob Wilson has been teaching, mentoring, coaching, and sharing principles concerning great money management and financial wisdom for more than 2 decades.

I believe that all the books in this wealth creation series will be a blessing to those who use them. This book in particular will be unique because it not only addresses what to do to manage wealth. It will also touch on who you want to become in the process. Bishop Bronner has also taught us the following:

If you become something disgusting and detestable in the process of reaching your goals, it is not worth it."

Rob Wilson cares about not only the money you accumulate but the character you emulate. Reading this book is a wise investment.

- Dr. Charles Houston
Pastor, Word of Faith Family Worship Cathedral

Preface

In October 2006, during my early years on radio, I had the pleasure of meeting Stephen M. R. Covey and interviewing him about his book "The Speed of Trust". What an experience for me, it changed everything about people and what I thought I knew about them.

It changed everything, how I acted, how I communicated my thoughts and vision. As the subtitle of his book says, it's the one thing that changes everything.

Trust is so underrated. Trust creates strong relationships and partnerships with people who can make a difference and allow you to make a difference, too.

Trust establishes a bond with others which allows one to not go through something alone. Trust or the lack of trust places a value on your action or the lack thereof.

It costs you dearly not to have, not just you but also whoever is involved with you. Mr. Covey explains in his book that mistrust is like an additional tax that you have to pay on everything. As I write about wealth creation and its place in the financial and investment industry there's one thing that cannot happen: break trust.

The financial industry and community banks have provided a place that should protect your hard-earned cash, a place where you could confidently go to discuss private financial information since the beginning. You trust your bank to do the right thing, day in and day out. When you walk in the bank, you trust that your banker will greet you with a smile, and when you are not there, you trust the bank to keep your personal information safe. Ultimately, you trust your bank to be there to help.

As I begin to write this book, "The Trust" of the series Wealth Creation, there are banks filing for bankruptcy, private banks providing over 80 billion dollars to rescue other community banks.

The trust of the community is being pushed to its limits, depositors are making a run on the banks taking their money out of the bank.

I pray that I am able to deliver to you my passion and honest views on how important trust is for you to create wealth.

Introduction

If you are reading "The Trust", I believe that you have read the other books of the series. I also believe that your mindset is/has changed to the point of understanding you are now a wealth creator. You are now entering into another level of wealth creation for you and your family.

A journey once to nowhere is now where you are becoming the first link to generational wealth transfer. But there are still some important hurdles you will have to overcome, hurdles that impact everything around you. It is trust.

Trust is an important factor in pretty much every relationship, including your relationship with yourself. Not trusting yourself can make it difficult to make decisions, trust your instincts, meet your needs, and make the most of opportunities.

Most of you never recognize there are signs that you don't trust yourself, why you might feel this way, how a lack of trust in yourself can impact you. Trusting your bank seems like a logical concept, right? Trusting your family members or friends, even trusting your employer should seem logical as well.

What I hope to establish are things you no longer take for granted when it comes to you trusting or developing trust. When you made the decision to create wealth, you decided that you wanted something so much different from average.

To be honest when you hear local or national news sources with headlines of banks found to have taken advantage of its customers makes you not trust banks. When it is fact, there are so many people who have always missed trusted banks and financial institutions.

This is why the very things that hinder wealth creation are the number of check cashiers, payday lending and other non-financial institutions. Lack of trust in yourself in the very first layer of mistrust. I want you to ponder these things as you read this book, look for what is impacting you the most and let's work on it.

Let's identify what may be signs of you not trust yourself:

- You seek reassurance and advice from others instead of tuning in to how you feel about a situation.
- You solicit opinions from others around you when an important decision must be made.
- You postpone making decisions and procrastinate as you find it easier to sit with uncertainty, compared to the fear that you made the wrong decision.
- You avoid tuning in to your needs and desires and disconnect instead.
- You overestimate the perspective of others and undervalue your own thoughts and instincts.

- You experience excessive guilt after making a decision and always fear that you've made the wrong choice.
- You ruminate on what could have been if you had taken another path.
- You compare your choices to others' decisions.
- You don't believe you've made a good decision unless you receive external validation.
- You are quick to believe negative opinions of yourself.
- You underestimate the power of your choices.
- You don't recognize and believe in your own innate value and worth.
- You often state that no one ever showed you how to save.

Not being able to trust yourself comes in all shapes and sizes from chronic self-doubt to indecisiveness and low self-esteem. You can experience pain from all those reason in the moment, but the real tragedy of all self-doubt is that it leads you to miss out on life:

- How many amazing careers were abandoned because people didn't trust themselves?
- How many incredible works of art never came to be because people didn't trust themselves?
- How many beautiful relationships never formed because people didn't trust themselves?

Sadly, many people's low self-trust goes unchecked and even gets worse over time because of one basic misunderstanding about what actually causes it. It's not events from your past that make it hard to trust yourself—it's your habits in the present.

You have for the most part created habits of sabotaging your self-trust, I want you to start trusting yourself more, so let's begin to work and eliminate them. The Trust

Chapter 1

Denying Self

End up at the wrong destination is simply ignoring the signs of denying self. Actually I should be saying it in a completely different way, like self-sabotaging is much different from looking the other way.

Denying yourself financially begins with you being in denial about your financial situation. Having financial struggles and tragedies is a result of everything involving you.

Financial upsets have come upon all of us at one point or another. Some of these upsets are graciously weathered while some are only swept under the carpet with the hope that they will all disappear on their own.

However, the ones that we hope will disappear into thin air keep most of us awake at night since they remain unresolved issues.

It is your financial issues that you have allowed to remain unresolved that your ability to fully achieve your short- and long-term financial goals is affected considerably. You will not, I repeat, you will not have the ability to create wealth.

One of the negative responses to a financial problem is denial. This is where you could have a money problem and you are unable to admit it. Since financial upsets do not often happen overnight, financial denial is built over many years.

How often have you failed to acknowledge the existence of a difficult situation in your financial life? I have clients who never accept the responsibility of being the cause of the problem or that it exists. You just do not slip into debt or denial and you certainly will not slip into wealth creation.

You cannot avoid facing the facts of a problem regardless of how much you are playing down the consequences of the issue at hand. Your delay in dealing with financial issues creates major financial problems down the road.

It may sound crazy, but I once read somewhere that financial denial as a type of money disorder where one tries as much as possible to not face the money problems head on and choose not to think about it at all.

You may have symptoms of this money disorder caused by financial denial, you know if you have been avoiding the reality about your financial situation. Here are a few clues;

- Underestimating your debt, i.e. failing to fully acknowledge the true amount that you owe
- Stuffing your bills and leaving them unopened
- You avoid checking your bank and mobile money statements
- You try as much as you can to not talk about money with friends and family

- Using lack of failure as evidence of success i.e. misconstruing 'luck' as evidence you are doing the right things
- Ignoring phone calls because you suspect that someone is reminding you about what you owe them
- You do not know what your net worth is
- You try to avoid thinking about money and finances
- Making 'someday' statements frequently
- Thinking emergencies won't happen to you
- Creatively making money problems look smaller than they really are
- Using success in one area of your life to overshadow failures

What is noteworthy is that denial, in all its forms, is the brain's defense mechanism where it rationalizes the mistakes you make to protect you. My theory is that in some cases, short-term denial could be all you need to get your life in order to adjust to a painful or stressful issue.

I have said in other books how this is mental and failure to accept responsibility does not make it go away. It is always that "what if" or "wasn't me" or "what happened was" form of thinking which elevates your crisis.

Because you are simply sticking your head in the sand you end up making the situation worse. When the situation gets worse, it brings out even more intense negative emotions which in turn lead to your denying the situation again. And on and on it goes. It's a vicious cycle.

Denying Self

You are aware of the vicious cycle you know when you have made mistakes in the past, and your brain is very good at helping you to not admit you have made a mistake. You will craft stories that make it someone else's fault.

You even attribute your mistakes to events outside of your control. When you have no other choice, the best way to avoid facing your reality is to simply not look.

I want to make sure that each of you readers understand what I am talking about is not targeted to any one group of people. So often, I have to convert non-readers to readers of my material, they do not see this as their issue. This is another person's problem. Yea right!

It's easy to think that this kind of phenomenon would happen to those who don't have much. After all, a lack of money tends to lead to money issues and stress. While that's true, a lack of money isn't a cause of financial denial.

You don't have to be poor, incompetent, impulsive, a shopaholic, or stupid to turn to financial denial. Many people who avoid thinking about their financial situations are very successful in other areas of their life.

They understand the need to make smart decisions with their money. Unfortunately, their money mindset gets in the way.

Wealth creation will not happen for you if you do not trust yourself. There is no foundation to build trust on when you place yourself in a sabotaging position all of the time.

You may be saying right now "not me", but who else other than you has control of your every thought. Who else?

Learning to be present, mindful, and aware of your financial situation is the first step toward making positive change in your financial life. Understand that it's not easy to change behavior, especially when the alternative is to face intense negative emotions.

If you are able to get to the point where you don't need to deny your anxiety, can recognize your negative emotions, and learn to be comfortable with doing the hard emotional work, your situation can gradually start to improve over time.

Even if this is not about wealth creation at this moment, for you take small steps, learn to recognize negative emotions, and pay attention to what needs to be done, and you'll make progress.

If you have a problem and fail to acknowledge it, nine times out of ten it comes back to bite you, hard!

And when it's about money, you want to make sure that you are well insured from any bites... LOL – BUT Live intentionally. I wrote a chapter about being intentionally intentional in the book Wealth Creation "The Focus".

Your finances affect every aspect of your life. People who are financially disciplined often have more control over their lives. I know most of you do not like the fact that budgeting is the first step to becoming financially responsible, but it is only a part of the battle. Cultivate good habits — like using your credit wisely and saying no to consumer debts — to ensure you stick to your budget.

Then you can begin saving and investing and before you know it you are on the path of establishing your financial foundation for wealth creation. I have to express to you that financial denial is as powerful as self-denial, it comes with a similar group of concerns.

Financial denial makes you feel better about your finances (or lack thereof) by not thinking about them. For many people like you this denial is a way to deal with stress and it manifests when you stop paying attention to your finances, not tracking them and not opening your statements.

Your money mindset, which is a set of individual beliefs regarding money and which shapes your decisions about how you earn, spend or invest your money will also have to change.

In my previous books you saw how your attitude towards money is one of the biggest determinants of your financial health. This includes how much you think you are worth, how much you think you can earn and what you can or cannot do with money. With that knowledge in mind, you should strive to go beyond your circumstances.

Financial denial comes with a lot of effort to cover up shame associated with one's financial situation or, even more often, the perceptions of oneself on account of where you are monetarily.

To deal with this, first start by truly assessing your situation through a financial self-audit to get a good picture of where you really are. Then gracefully accept that this is where you are at today and understand that your situation does not mean you are lazy or stupid.

Your financial denial is the get-in debt stress coping mechanism, deal with it by paying attention to your finances, tracking them and going through your financial statements. Failure to do this can be destructive to your financial wellbeing.

You have to create routines that help you steer clear from acts of denial such as daily financial journaling, budgeting, money-related to-do lists.

Financial denial becomes your coping mechanism and the real issue can only be dealt with when you can step back a bit and evaluate your situation which can ultimately lead to success.

Evaluate the blame and your situation as much as possible to finally start on your way out of the current financial circumstance.

Recently I have been working with a client, this client is facing financial challenges from a number of perspectives. Her struggle often pushes her towards creating new debt in order to try and cover her denial.

When you decide that you will not accept responsibility for your actions, it is hard to remedy your situation, you must take full accountability and responsibility for your situation and then seek advice from a trusted confidante so you can improve your situation.

At the core of financial denial is financial illiteracy which more often than not can lead to money mismanagement and debt. Since negative money matters can lead to a lower self-esteem, reduced productivity and stress, they are too important to ignore.

TRUST is about knowledge and it goes without saying that you have to keep building your financial literacy skills by learning through formal means, from peers of groups and, importantly, practicing the learning day to day. GET OUT OF YOUR OWN WAY

Some will say it is never that serious, when push comes to shove over your finances, remember to always be easy on yourself. You can adopt the use of automated systems to help you with planning how your money is spent, saved or invested.

Have automatic reminders for the due date of bills etc. to ease your burden of remembering things.

Ignoring a prevailing financial problem not only hurts your peace of mind but blinds you from opportunities to move past the current hurdle since you are effectively doing nothing about it and somehow expecting the universe to solve it for you.

The good thing is that when you take the single step of accepting that a problem exists, you can open up your mind to considering solutions and actually relieve some of the mental pressure that comes with the knowledge that you have unresolved money issues.

Self-denial is your biggest challenge to trust. If you want to start trusting yourself more, look out for these subtle habits sabotaging your self-trust and work to eliminate them.

Remember that this situation of not being able to trust yourself comes in all shapes and sizes from chronic self-doubt and indecisiveness and low self-esteem.

These things are painful and the real tragedy of all self-doubt is that it leads you to miss out on your best life. Please understand it's not events from your past that make it hard to trust yourself—it's your habits in the present.

On the other hand, one of the best ways to start rebuilding trust in yourself is to have the courage—yes, sometimes it takes courage!—to follow your curiosity and pursue the things you are authentically interested in, even if it goes against the grain of what society or your spouse or whoever thinks.

If you're constantly reminding yourself that you're a screw-up, is it any surprise that you have a hard time trusting yourself? If you want to trust yourself more, live your life going forward, not in reverse.

"In the process of letting go you will lose many things from the past, but you will find yourself."

Denying Self

I know that you can rebuild the trust in yourself and make the changes that are necessary. You now must see that your life is full of routine and habit, and in many ways, that's good. A routine of things you do day in and day out, helps you accomplish a lot without having to think too much about it.

These become automatic responses as you go from one activity/event to another. If you had to think about all of the things you do in one day over and over again as if it were the first time you were doing them, you'd be wasting a lot of time and energy.

So conserving time by not focusing on the negative and using your energy feeling good about yourself on an ongoing basis is adaptive and practical, helps you get through what you need to do, and frees you up for the very important things you need to focus on. This is when you can build your confidence and move more and more back towards trusting you. It's all about Wealth Creation.

Chapter Two

Instinct

How often were you told to "Just trust your instinct," or "Just trust your gut," but what does it actually mean and more importantly, how do you do it?

I have written many books and articles on wealth and wealth creation, I have always tried to drive home the idea (I'm coming back to the idea) and the fact that it's all about mindset. But wait, could it be about something else, could it be that the mindset is the force behind a thing?

What is this thing? It's your gut instinct, or intuition. With your gut you are immediately able to understand something; there's no need to think it over or get another opinion—you just know.

Your intuition arises as a feeling within your body that only you experience. Because the feeling is so personal, no one else can weigh in to tell you if you're in touch with your gut instinct or not. You alone have to make the call. Because of this, trusting your intuition is the ultimate act of trusting yourself.

Wealth creation becomes a level four operation, you are about to enter into another space of your journey and you are going to have to listen to your intuition for it to help you avoid bad decisions and financial relationships.

Throughout your life, many people will have ideas about what's best for you, some held with good intentions and some coming from a place of deceitful, harmful, selfish intent.

Guts

Times like when your cousin discovered that your tax check was deposited, they come up with ways to benefit themselves.

To be honest here it's sometimes hard to tell which category someone falls into, but if you put aside all of those external opinions and instead listen to the advice of your own intuition, it may be able to guide you to what is truly best for you.

Making the best investment decision, selecting the best bank, determining the process of making tough choices is not always easy. You might feel as if you don't have enough time or information to develop or create the right strategy.

Even when the mindset is not present, no matter what you go through, your body will give you specific signs. You will have hunches regarding everything you do. And it's very tempting to listen to those hunches. But it's not always recommended.

Sometimes you have to resort to logic and rationale. Sometimes, there's no better way of getting through life than following your instincts. I did so the majority of my life; it was my instincts that pushed me to move forward.

You cannot be a nervous wreck as you strive to be a wealth creator. Making new financial decisions on investments, savings and retirement will trigger your first instincts to manifest either physically or emotionally.

Depending on what your gut is trying to tell you, your body will behave differently. Thus, the signals you will get will take on different forms.

There are two sides to the whole first instincts story I have been told. They will either alert you to be cautious or confirm the choices you want to make. Sounds simple enough!

Everything with money often creates sensations similar to those associated with anxiety, including the physical ones. You might feel dizzy, sick to your stomach. You might sweat or tremble. Always the uncertainty will hover around your mind, nagging and stressing you out.

I know that some of you after reading the other books in this series are feeling like you should be cautious, your hunches are evoking as if you are about to do something wrong.

Now you want to walk away, give up, quit the process, but when you react this way, you better run as far as possible from your denial.

On the other hand, you might feel confirmation from your instincts. An overwhelming sense of calm and confidence might take over you for apparently no reason. While there is no identifiable logical reason, it's your body telling you to pursue a particular course of action.

The feelings of affirmation are less physical. Often, you have to be in touch with your emotions to distinguish upbeat hunches. You may even seem to "hear" your gut talking to you and guiding you through decision-making processes.

I do not ever recall any of my wealthy mentors explaining to me how exactly these gut feelings work, and why they manifest around wealth creation.

Sometimes it may seem to come out of nowhere, they aren't actually all that random. As the name might suggest, gut feelings (instincts) have some connection with the gut.

"Wealth Creation may not be the mindset, it may take guts." – Rob Wilson

There is a gut-brain connection that I believe your feelings come into alignment and because of this connection, emotional experiences emerge, anxiety, fear, concern might lead to pain, stomach spasms, and nausea.

Even the positive feelings are expressed outwards in specific physical ways. Again, twinges, known commonly as "butterflies," are a widespread expression.

So trusting yourself in all areas of your life and not just about money can be important. Talking about instincts you always have to look out for certain misjudgments. The one that can hurt you the most is the first instinct misjudgment, and you always stick to the first option, you are at higher risk of being wrong.
Know the difference and be careful and don't listen to your first instincts because they were the hunches you got first. That's deceptive thinking.

Instead, use those hunched combined with logic to reach a decision. It would help if you learned which situations can be solved with logic and in which you can lean only on instincts.

I hope that I am bringing you some understanding why you have gut instincts and spot them, you need to know when to trust them.

You have to trust your first instincts when forming first impressions of people, money and locations. In situations where you have just met someone, you won't have enough real data to decide what you really think of the person accurately.

What you will know is if it is worth seeing them again. Would it be to your advantage to spend resources trying to build a relationship with them? How exactly should you approach the situation?

This is exactly what I want you to realize. Your first look at stocks, bonds and mutual funds will be that you do know enough about them. You will or should know that this is a relationship that you desire and you will pursue it in every way.

In relationships, especially new ones, you should lean on instincts to guide you. Don't use logic to analyze whether to pursue a financial relationship you might use misleading discerning.

Because it is easy to not value new things, you could easily tend to distance yourself from new opportunities. It's almost understandable because you don't want to risk investing resources if you don't envision a guaranteed good outcome.

In my next book (The Speed) I will be talking about various ways to create investment products and protect yourself 100% guaranteed. This will be new for most of you, however, you will still dismiss it because logic may tell you that it's not possible to invest and not lose something.

Your gut may guide you in these situations. Don't lean on logic, as you will stumble over misjudgment.

Instead, listen to your emotions. If something you have just learned makes you feel uneasy, even though it is praised by others, it's better to back off.

Your logic might tell you to pursue a relationship because you have heard many good things. But that will not turn out well. Your gut knows better. You don't have enough information to decide rationally, so there's no other tool you could use but instincts.

Whenever you need to form a quick decision, always resort to gut instincts. Don't listen to others, don't try to make logical assumptions. Take a step back and understand what you feel, and work from there.

Sometimes, you have enough data to make a logical and reasonable decision. But that doesn't mean you are sure about the validity of what you've decided. The anxiety caused by not being 100% certain can even make you turn back on your decision.

It can make you procrastinate, put you under a lot of pressure. There are some situations in which no amount of logic will boost your confidence. If that's the case, you can rely on instincts to give you the boost you need.

The brain registers everything you've ever done. Subconsciously, you have a significant amount of experience. But you aren't aware of that knowledge. Based on events that have happened, your brain can guide you through the best plan possible.

If you're ever in doubt, listen to your instincts. The subconscious will show you what's right and what's wrong by giving you signals. If your decision is the right one, you will feel no anxiety. Your instincts will make you feel secure and comfortable. But, if the decision is wrong, you will feel nothing but fear regarding your plan.

Be aware that you can decide whatever you need to fix. Understand that your life experiences sharpen your instincts and guide you along the way. If you become aware of this fact, you will learn to listen to your instincts and trust your decisions.

That's not to say you should make decisions based only on instincts. Instead, create a logical plan first and only use instincts to confirm if that plan is correct or not.

Now in the previous point, you've just read how instincts shouldn't be the foundation for decision-making. And that is very true for cases in which you have time to decide. But the reality is that sometimes you don't have that time.

You can't sit around for hours on end to craft the perfect course of action. It would be best if you decided on the spot. You have at best a few minutes and at worst a split second. What do you do in that case?

Maybe just maybe you should base your decisions on intuition alone. If you're in imminent danger, it's useless to try to think your way out of it. If you're going to fall off the bike straight on your head, thinking will do you no good. Instead, your instincts will rightfully tell you that you should jump rather than break your neck.

Instincts are the best way to find the right path in a time crunch. And, as a bonus, instincts will get you in touch with your needs. When you don't have time to sit back and analyze the context, you won't logically identify them.

But your decisions need to take your needs into account. If your instincts tell you something, the chances are that's what's best for you. Trust!

The first thoughts your brain will have will always be the ones that bring you the most benefits. When your instincts tell you to jump off the bike so that you don't break your neck, it's because it's best for you. Even if you risk hitting someone, your instinct will still tell you to save yourself.

So many people end up broke and discuss only because they dismissed their first thoughts and took on too much debt or allowed the broke cousin to use the credit card and go on vacation. It is very likely that instinct was ignored.

And even in more minor extreme examples, the situation stays the same. If you need to decide on an answer to a proposal in a couple of minutes, your instincts will have your best interests at heart.

Listening carefully to these instincts has had a pretty bad reputation in the past. People who follow them have been accused of being irrational and flaky. But that couldn't be further from the truth. Though logic is vital in all aspects of life, instincts have their role.

So yes, you should trust your first instincts. It would help if you didn't base every decision you make on your first instincts. But, in certain situations, instincts are the critical aspect.

I wonder about what the wealthy 3% feel about instincts over logic? Wow, that is it – you just experienced your first instinct at its core best.

So, what is your answer?

Instincts, or gut feelings, are clear signs. They create physical, or at least emotional, reactions. So, there's no way you won't be aware of your instincts in every situation. There are three main times in which listening to your first instincts are recommended.

Firstly, take instincts into account when forming a first impression. Like when you meet someone, there's no guarantee they are the way they seem. If you feel uneasy, take that into account.

Secondly, use instincts for confirmation. To make sure your decisions are the right ones, listen to your gut. If you feel comfortable, the decision doesn't need tweaking. But, if your instincts tell you that something is off, maybe take another look.

Lastly, use first instincts when having to make quick plans.

Instincts will subconsciously guide you, and they will take care of your needs. When you have a few minutes or a split second to decide, it's useless to try to think it through.

Gut feelings are the best way to go. As long as you learn to balance listening to logic and first instincts, you should trust your gut!

Guts

SEE IT THROUGH!

When you're up against a trouble,
   Meet it squarely, face to face;
Lift your chin and set your shoulders,
   Plant your feet and take a brace.
When it's vain to try to dodge it,
   Do the best that you can do;
You may fail, but you may conquer,
   See it through!

Black may be the clouds about you
   And your future may seem grim,
But don't let your nerve desert you;
   Keep yourself in fighting trim.
If the worst is bound to happen,
   Spite of all that you can do,
Running from it will not save you,
   See it through!

Even hope may seem but futile,
   When with troubles you're beset,
But remember you are facing
   Just what other men have met.
You may fail, but fall still fighting;
   Don't give up, whatever you do;
Eyes front, head high to the finish.
   See it through!   By Edgar A. Guest

Chapter Three

Awareness

You must be aware of the things that impact you in every area of your life. As a wealth creator, your awareness of your decision making is critical. Not only do you need to trust yourself, you have to trust others and new processes.

I know that you have felt very sure that you couldn't trust someone even if they had never done anything to cause you to doubt them. You simply don't.

There may be something going with you and trust issues. Trust issues can cause suspicion, anxiety, and doubt, and can be very damaging to personal and financial relationships.

It is my opinion that trust issues have much to do with your security concerns. Who/what is it around you, what are they bringing to the table that may sabotage your ability to create wealth.

My first trust issues with money came when I was twelve years of age. I watched people scam and hustle money from people every day, some of them were aware that they had been hustled yet they would return only to be hustled again.

You may have awareness of situations which cause you to mistrust others around you. You may even seem deceptive with money while growing up that it has shaped how you think about money and investments today.

Awareness

Awareness financially is about you being present. I remember being on a high level call back in 2021 and a part of the discussion really had me in a different mindset. It caused me to see an approach with your financial life/framework and assuming that your resource or your plans has already been compromised.

When you take such an approach it's like you are validating your process based on your awareness and strategy. The trust you should have behind your financial framework is you being present so that everyone is on the same playing field.

And just because your financial framework requires validating doesn't mean that you don't trust your family, it means trust but verify.

You can trust your family (spouse/children or other) to do the right thing while also putting a safety net in place and being aware. It's like when you ride as a passenger in a car, you wear your seatbelt—not because you don't trust the driver (maybe), but because there are so many variables that could cause an accident. And you want to be safe if an accident occurs.

With financial awareness, you are doing your household a favor. You are all on the same page, working to ensure your wealth creation and your most vital assets will remain secure.

Being present (awareness) enables just that.

Let me point out to you that taking steps to be present, mindful, and aware of your financial situation is the first step toward making positive change in your financial life. Understand that it's not easy to change behavior, especially when the alternative is to face intense negative emotions.

If you are able to get to the point where you don't need to deny your anxiety, can recognize your negative emotions, and learn to be comfortable with doing the hard emotional work, your situation can gradually start to improve over time. It's like saving $19.56 a week, in one year you will save over a thousand dollars.

It is hard to trust yourself when you are not present in any area of your life. I have talked about financial denial, and the tendency you have to ignore your personal financial situation.

Being aware may seem frightening, so to ignore it makes it easier to deal with the emotional discomfort that comes along with the state of your finances. It is a fact that people who are unaware often ignore their finances as a way to avoid thinking about it.

- Not looking at statements, bills, or accounts
- Trying hard to forget about your financial situation
- Avoiding thinking about money
- Not talking about money, even when it's necessary
- Not saving for the future
- Denying negative feelings about money

Even though it seems like a good idea in the short run, it doesn't do us any good in the long run.

Sometimes you just know you have made mistakes in the past, and your brains are very good at helping you to not admit you have made a mistake.

Are like many others who will acknowledge they had something else in focus and it really was a mistake more like a slip up. SAME THING!

Sometimes you even craft stories that make it someone else's fault. Sometimes you attribute your mistakes to events outside of our control. When you have no other choice, the best way to avoid facing your reality is to simply not look.

No, I want you aware, mindful of the challenges that you once had and trusting yourself first.

Let yourself practice trusting in small, safe ways. I know that you are working on you, but take someone at their word. Give them the benefit of the doubt. Start allowing yourself time if your trust was broken.

Be aware if your trust has been broken, it's going to take some time without further betrayal for the person to earn it back. If someone is genuine in wanting to build trust again, they will respect this process. I want you to be careful not to accuse or blame.

Instead, communicate clearly how you are feeling and what you need. Spend some time thinking, journaling, or talking to a friend about your wealth creation goals and you trust in yourself to have power to change your life.

With you acknowledging your trust issues is a necessary component to getting over it. Rather than blaming others or deflecting the issue, take responsibility for your situation.

Acknowledging the issue does not mean that you have to accept or like it. It only means that you understand the presence of an issue, and you are willing to fight it.

Even with money or without it, the fight is the fight. Remember, trust that is broken it's not caused by lack of money, it's easy to think it would happen to those who don't have much.

After all, a lack of money tends to lead to money issues and stress.

Yes, yes, that's true, a lack of money isn't a cause of financial denial. You don't have to be poor, incompetent, impulsive, a shopaholic, or stupid to turn to financial denial.

Get this, many people who avoid thinking about their financial situations are very successful in other areas of their life. They understand the need to make smart decisions with their money. Unfortunately, their money mindset gets in the way.

Awareness trust believes in the integrity of yourself and others. The real deal behind building trust means that you feel secure in your interactions and relationships with people and money, and are able to be open and vulnerable about it.

Look at it this way when people harm you and betray your trust, your feeling of security can be shattered. You start to expect the worst from others and become suspicious and skeptical.

This lack of trust, commonly referred to as having trust issues, can be very harmful to your mental health, your relationships with others and wealth creation.

Make wealth creation a shared, cross-functional process so that it will spark engagement among your family or partner. If you are able to get their engagement and buy-in you're building a network that can educate, build trust, and influence wealth creation in ways that are unimaginable.

Awareness

Create a regular rhythm of engagement and seeking feedback, you want to keep wealth creation at the top of mind at all times, not just when your resources are plentiful your awareness should be all the time.

Mindfulness practice is another way to bring awareness to whatever to your efforts of wealth creation. Even if it's too time-consuming to do this for many of the activities you do during the day, stop for one or two activities to be totally present.

That could be going for a walk after dinner, or a morning jog, or it could be doing the dishes. The idea is to be totally engaged in every aspect of the activity.

Instead of thinking a thousand thoughts and doing your activity by routine, bring your full awareness to every aspect of what you're doing. Give it the time and energy it deserves. See the importance in everything you do.

Another way to be present in the moment is to set an intention. Man did I talk about this already in the last book "The Focus".

Why are you doing anything other than the fact that you have to? By setting an intention, you're stating why this activity is necessary and giving it meaning.

Last chapter I spoke about you using your instinct, your gut. Now allow your awareness to use your senses to ground you. I know this may sound too simplistic but it's actually a wonderful way to approach being present in any given moment.

Since so much of what you do is mentally motivated, inevitably what your senses are picking up is often taken for

26

granted. But your senses alert you and inform you about what is going on around you, at least on an unconscious level.

So practice paying attention to what you see, smell, hear, taste, and touch. In fact, this works particularly well when you're feeling anxious and/or depressed. Stop what you're thinking and consciously feel what your senses are bringing to your attention.

Allow me to shift gears a little bit. I am talking about trust and using awareness as one of the keys to trust. I am also talking about wealth creation and the trust and awareness in your day to day life in dealing with finance.

Financial awareness is more important than you may think. Plus, what's more fun than financial independence? First off, think about that great feeling you get when you don't have the looming specter of debt hanging over you.

Also, sound financial decisions can really make a difference down the road. Remember, retirement is a time to take all those vacations you couldn't when you were working the daily grind.

Because money is important to your overall peace of mind, financial awareness, trust awareness makes it necessary to review where you are now and where you're going financially. Don't let bad financial decisions ruin the best years of your life!

I believe that teaching you how to trust new processes as well as embracing a new awareness to allow you to discover even more resources to help with your financial, estate and gift planning financial awareness, and the essential principles to smart money wealth creation are very important as this gives you the tools of empowerment to make better informed everyday money decisions so you can:

- Live a quality life without outliving your wealth
- Watch your personal / family dreams become a reality
- Make decisions about your lifestyle without financial worry
- Enjoy a financially secure, debt-free future
- Work with financial professionals and product providers to get the best results for your time and money
- Pass on values, knowledge and assets to future generations to make their lives and this world a better place

This gives you the tools to address everyday wealth creation decisions and trust them in a more informed manner and have the best possibilities to reach and maintain your personal and family financial goals, financial freedom and security; while passing on values, knowledge and assets to future generations to make their lives better.

Most of my readers are aspiring business people with brilliant ideas and have started their own companies. They have several areas of expertise that are required to make their business a sustained successful venture.

The entrepreneurship in them shows that they may be very knowledgeable about the business domain, how to recruit skilled manpower, design business strategies, and plan product's marketing initiatives.

However, if they are unable to handle the various financial aspects of the business, they are sure to fail.

Similarly, if your household is not prudent about managing your finances, how much ever they earn as income will not be sufficient to bring financial stability.

You will always end up spending more than you earn. And during emergencies such as in the present times, you will face a lot of hardships without contingency funds for such situations.

The basic idea behind both these scenarios is the importance of financial awareness. A few important aspects of financial awareness are listed below to help an individual/entrepreneur in their short and long-term plans.

As I close awareness, yes trust awareness and financial awareness helps you to achieve a balance between profitability and security of your wealth creation. I can't stress on this point often enough.

The importance of planning for unforeseen difficulties, loss of income, health emergencies, monetary shortfall – this is the biggest lesson that the pandemic has taught us.

Whether it is getting adequate life/health insurance, or keeping aside emergency funds in some easily accessible instrument, you have to work out their own contingency plans.

And these plans vary depending on your household. Your awareness will be your power to trust your decisions.

You are worthy!

I've heard it said that self-worth comes from within.

To feel strong and true, you must be content with where you've been.

It's so tempting to look around, to compare yourself to others, and measure your worth by what you've found.

But you're more than a number.

You're more than the sum of what happened to you in the past.

You are more than the mistakes that you've made.

You are more than the words people say when they don't know how to love you, or just don't care enough to try.

Chapter Four

Self-Confidence

Wealth creation is going to involve you understanding that it is not just about having money, it is about understanding you. Do you have self-trust?

Recently one of my younger clients was full of energy and excitement for a new job opportunity he did not trust. An opportunity that would easily pay him mid six figures, yet he did not move forward on the job offer.

When I question why, he informs me that he lacks the confidence to do the job. His knowledge and education makes him qualified for the position, he cannot imagine himself doing his job at that level. Trusting yourself becomes your personal asset or your personal kryptonite.

As a wealth creator, you are growing at every level. Some of your challenges have more to do with your upbringing and your DNA. The things that have impacted you and have denied you financial growth are from within.

Self-trust is you having confidence in your skills, choices, and values. It comes from within you and feels like an inner knowing of your strengths and weaknesses while still thinking positively about yourself.

Whether it's paying off a student loan, credit card, or covering your basic expenses each month—feeling financially confident means different things to different people. What can make us feel financially confident as individuals can also change throughout our lifetime, and is shaped by our evolving needs.

Growth

Having self-confidence comes from the information and ideas you take in through the world that support a positive perspective about you. It is stated that often you enter into the world with an abundance of self-confidence.

Consider the young child who feels confident taking risks like jumping off the swings or dances without a care in front of a crowd. When you are a young child and affirmed and encouraged, you strengthen your sense of self and begin to hold cognitive schemas that confirm you are worthy, valuable, beautiful, intelligent, etc.

The fact is even though you can have a strong sense of confidence as a child, life will often throw curve balls that can diminish confidence.

Creating low self-confidence can feel like being unable to handle other people's criticisms or difficulty trusting yourself and others. Not able to trust yourself with money and finance.

Wealth creation is in your sight path now and you have to believe and know that the great thing is, every moment is a chance to build evidence toward your self-confidence.

To make up for what was lost, you can rebuild confidence over time through small and large moments that ladder up toward more self-trust, more growth.

It is like creating your own financial ladder, I am getting a book ahead of myself. Imagine opening an investment account of some kind. You know that you only have a limited amount of money to invest, so you start with what you have and build from there.

Every month you will start making a deposit of $88 into an account or you could use the weekly method of $19.76 a week until you can build up a higher deposit. Overtime, you will see your savings or investments begin to grow. These small but consistent steps begin to build confidence in saving and investing.

Your trust in your ability as a wealth creator and just as you can build positive self-confidence, there are things that can and will erode it.

Look, it's like a target on your back at first or it may even be the way you are socializing and seen by those around you, in addition to difficult transitions in your childhood, adolescence, and now adulthood, can all lead to lower self-confidence.

You must grow, please by all means necessary grow. You will have varying levels of confidence that can also show up in different situations. You may feel very confident in earning money because you were socialized and praised to succeed in your career.

You may feel less confident when it comes to purchasing stocks because you've previously received criticisms from peers and haven't yet processed their feedback in a useful way.

There is always good news and that is low self-confidence is fixable, and you are totally in charge of making it happen. I need you to believe in you.

When you can identify the root cause for low self-confidence it can provide a map of how to build up more positive self-confidence. A good place to start is through self-reflection and journaling.

Growth

Wealth creation will get scary at times, by self-reflection it helps you remain and build on a steady pace of growth. As you try to get to the possible root cause of your low self-confidence one thing to do is begin to record any low self-confidence thoughts or sayings that keep showing up for you.

It's important for you as each thought or saying happens, ask yourself "Who or what told you that?" Decide if you want to allow that voice to have authority over your thoughts in this stage of your life. Journal out your reactions and create a plan of action to move forward.

You know that feeling you get when you earn or win money, especially that unexpected money. It is such a feeling of freedom of expression, feeling of joy and most importantly it is a feeling of satisfaction. When trust is high there is this feeling and it is different from anyone else's.

You must understand what self-confidence feels like for you. If you do not know, take some time to figure out what confidence feels like in your body. A good question to ask is "How will you know that you've reached a satisfactory level of self-confidence?"

Perhaps you will start speaking up more. You might finally wear that outfit you've always wanted to. You may even introduce yourself to your crush at your co-working space. You will take investment classes.

This will be different from person to person, so it doesn't have to make sense to anyone else. This is your personal measurement of confidence and growth.

There needs to be an alignment with yourself, your values and your vision about wealth creation and yourself give you power. Consider this, if you find yourself frequently using the word "should," (for example, I should have been married by 30, I should have a house by next year, or I should have my life together by now, I should be out of debt), take a step back and reflect. Where is this "should" coming from?

Too many of the "shoulds" in life stem from cultural or familial expectations placed on you. With all of these statements, it's helpful to always ask yourself: Is this what I truly want for myself? You have the power to reclaim your life at any point.

The more that you make decisions aligned with your true self and your desires, the more confident you will become in your decision-making.

Even with a wealthy mindset, having a growth mindset encourages you to explore beyond your current skills and knowledge, keeping the possibility of improvement open. Instead of using phrases like "I'm not confident," just add "yet" to it, which transforms the old belief into "I'm not confident yet."

This adds the qualifier that you are in the process of gaining skills to become confident.

Trust, (LOL) trust me when I tell you that a growth mindset intervention will lead to better saving and investments when you are immersed in environments that encourage growth mindset principles. So it's worth exploring your new growth mindset with like-minded people.

Trusting yourself also helps you know you will fail, and that's OK. You know we live in a failure-averse culture where people mostly just talk about their accomplishments.

Growth

Rarely do you ever get to hear about people's accounts of failure. With you understanding that failure happens and is a part of the process of living will help you to live more fully.

For a lot of you, you were usually taught that self-confidence comes from achievements. However, this means that when you achieve, you feel great about your abilities, but when you fail, your self-confidence takes a hit.

I truly believe that self-confidence comes from your own thoughts about your abilities rather than external achievements. So that regardless of whether you succeed or fail, you have the power to retain your self-confidence."

Sometimes you might hesitate to trust yourself because you've received critical feedback from authority figures earlier in life, like parents, teachers, or community leaders, and you have adopted their criticisms as your own beliefs. But there comes a point when this feedback no longer serves your current life.

Standing up to those old criticisms can unlock a new level of confidence. Your confidence can also be built by rewriting the narratives in your heads about your worthiness. This involves identifying self-limiting beliefs and reframing them.

Often the voice in your head that tells you are not good enough is not your authentic voice but a total of all the voices of those who have criticized you in the past. When you talk back to the inner critic enough, the confident inner-child that you lost touch with can reemerge."

Keep in mind that your emotions go through a cycle of beginning, middle, and end. Although emotions can feel really intense in the moment, they are only temporary. At the very basic level, emotions are functional responses to motivations in your environment.

In terms of confidence, any emotion like anxiety, stress, or fear that is holding you back from taking action is only temporary. Once it subsides, you can make your next move. As the saying goes, "Feel the fear and do it anyway."

Wealth creation will be found in the focus and trust in what you can control. A lot of times, you have to base your self-confidence on things you actually have no control over—what other people think, the outcome of a project, others' reactions, etc...

To build self-confidence, you need to release your attachment to the things you can't control and start basing your self-confidence on what you do have control over.

Another process to build self-confidence against things you don't have control over, focus on the things you can control—for example, how prepared you are, your passion for the presentation topic, and how much work you've put into it.

Remind yourself of these things consistently and repeatedly until they become your new beliefs!

Grounding yourself in things you can control, even just one aspect of your goal, will provide you with more stability to move forward.

And remember: Building confidence builds more confidence. By starting in the places you have control over, you can ensure that you build confidence from a place of inner strength.

Growth

You have heard the saying many times, if you are the smartest person in your circle then you are in the wrong circle. If nine of your closest friends are broke it is like that you will be number 10. You have to build a like-minded community around you.

Listen, your views of yourself are usually inaccurate. Whether you underestimate or overestimate your abilities, you can't create a more accurate level of self-confidence in isolation. You need to interact with your environment, hobbies, and other people to build confidence.

Sharing your experience with a few close friends who are on the same wealth creation journey will be valuable. Find resources in your community like coaches, podcasts, blogs, and books to help build a foundation for your new confidence. Be sure you read all of the Wealth Creation series.

Cultivating a sense of self-compassion can help you to sympathize with yourself when you experience difficulties in life. This can help you turn away from negative, demeaning self-talk and toward more loving, nurturing ways to talk to yourself.

Compassion is key in cultivating self-confidence, holding on to past 'mistakes' or 'failures' really affects how confident you are. If you can be kind to yourself and allow yourself to let go of these moments, then you allow yourself to trust yourself.

There are many ways to build self-confidence. One approach involves processing and uprooting the formative experiences that may have contributed to a negative sense of self.

There are great benefits in boosting your confidence while it may feel unnatural and like a lot of work, there are plenty of benefits of building self-confidence or self-trust.

Wealth creation may be new to you, saving and investing, stocks and bonds, but it is important for you to build resilience to try new things. Confidence is the life source for much of what you seek in life. It gives you the fuel you need to try new things and take risks.

Think about it, you actually have better performance whether it's at work, in sports, or in personal endeavors, having confidence helps you accomplish tasks with more ease and, therefore, success.

Confidence in one area can beget confidence in other areas. Confidence has even been proven to be a higher predictor of performance than competence!

Creating the life you want as a wealth creator begins now if it hasn't already. When you don't believe in yourself, you tend to take actions that actually create the exact outcome you fear. By boosting your self-confidence, you can take actions and create outcomes that better reflect the incredible power that's within you.

Remember, you can be good at a lot of things, but with self-confidence, you'll be able to determine which things you want to become good at, not just build confidence in the things you get external praise for. This is where making your own decisions according to your true self.

When you're confident in yourself, you start making decisions that are in line with what you truly want. You listen less to the well-meaning advice around you telling you what you should do and you start doing things that you truly want to do.

While most of us are born with a healthy level of confidence, life throws us challenges that can derail our sense of confidence.

However, reclaiming that self-confidence is possible and worth every effort for living a more fulfilling life. Trust changes the speed of everything.

Chapter Five

Transparency

I think the real currency of your journey to wealth creation is transparency. You've got to be truthful. I don't think you should be vulnerable every day and everyone, but there are moments where you've got to share your soul and conscience with people and show them who you are, and not be afraid of it.

Listen, everyone around you has their own truth, waiting for a safe space to emerge. When you open up to sharing your truth from a place of curiosity, you become that safe space, and that allows more truth to emerge.

Being authentic and transparent allows you to be at ease with yourself, to speak and act with integrity, and to be trustworthy for others, inspiring them to speak more truth as well.

Especially as leader of your household, you have to be the first to speak your truth. You have to do it consistently and courageously, or it simply will not feel safe for others.

Most of you will wonder why and how am I trying to empower you as a wealth creator talking about being authentic and transparent when it comes to your personal finance and wealth creation. There is a lot for you to pull from this if you are serious about your wealth creation journey.

Transparency

Being authentic and transparent for me as I write this chapter will even challenge me to be just that. Ironically as I write this, there is a gospel song playing in my background with the chorus line saying something like "I wasn't created to worry, I wasn't created to fear". How appropriate for this chapter message to you.

You being authentic and transparent takes a lot of courage. Not everyone can show their true motives or true self because of fear. Fear of judgments. Fear of being rejected. Fear of being less authoritative. And sometimes, fear of being manipulated. Worry!

I know that transparency builds trust, trust that leads to better communication, fewer personal issues, and many other benefits. If you are honest, truthful, and transparent, people trust you.

If people trust you, you have no grounds for fear, suspicion or jealousy. "Transparency is important – all things. More than its significance, transparency is good, and we all need it.

Transparency means not having anything to hide, which is so much different from having things that should be kept private or confidential. It means embracing all of yourself – your shadow and your light – and living as that person, as your whole self, in your personal, professional and financial life.

You would not believe the number of people whose financial life has stalled because of the lack of transparency. Either they have no trust in the system or they believe in the system and fear rejection.

The person, who has something to hide, has something to hurt. It isn't that people set out to hurt you, but what you try to hide, or refuse to accept within yourself, becomes a trigger, easily set off by whatever is going on around you. It also creates an energy of distrust that people feel, intuitively, whether they are conscious of it or not.

Whatever you try to keep behind your mask (your figurative mask, not Covid mask) actually becomes more visible. Let's say you see someone talking down to others while bragging about themselves.

It doesn't take much to realize that their arrogance is a mask, hiding insecurities about their own worthiness. By trying to hide them, those insecurities actually become glaring red flags, continually on display.

I so often encounter people that immediately begin to brag about themselves as soon as they hear that I am a financial coach. They share what they in most cases do not have in their investment portfolio, and turn to ask me my thoughts about what they have.

On the other hand, if that same person were honest with themselves about their inner struggles, their finances, spoke to themselves with kindness, and out loud said occasional things like, "I hope I'm doing the right thing here.

I sometimes worry about that." … Wouldn't your image of them change? We'd no longer see them as insecure, but as

Transparency

honest, strong and human. They would be much more at peace with themselves as well.

Let me ask you... When you hear "transparency", what comes to mind?

I get many questions from many different people. Of course, every situation is unique and there will be different kinks and quirks to work through.

But, there are some general guidelines for transparency that can help you start exploring the benefits, even if you're the only one on board (for now).

If you've already begun practicing transparency, see this as guidance for how to improve transparency in your family as well as wealth creation.

I really like this definition: "Transparency means establishing congruence between who you say you are and who you really are. It means walking your talk."

That's what's at the heart of financial transparency. It's owning who you are with love, and showing up as that person, so that your energy can be directed towards something better than hiding what makes you human.

When you are hiding something it turns into more than insecurities. Often, you hide your true strengths, talents, values and purpose because we feel uncomfortable or afraid.

44

You worry about what people will say or about opening a box that can't be closed again. If it is your wealth creation, don't lose sight.

When you hide these things, you aren't bringing your best selves forward. Not only can your family suffer as a result, your well-being and happiness suffer as well, as do our relationships with the people around you.

It also isn't just arrogance that you hide behind. Not speaking up, people pleasing, procrastinating, impatience with others, staying in your comfort zone... all of these things are "mask behaviors". They are things you do to hide your true selves and stay safe. The problem is, safe means stuck, safe means being broke.

Wealth creation and transparency fosters authentic relationships. Being open makes you less intimidating and more approachable, bringing you closer to your resources.

You become more authentic and human than a person simply surviving. Thus, allowing transparency to set a foundation for a healthy investment relationship and a positive mindset.

People trust you more. Openness and honesty are powerful traits. You can't expect people to trust you right away. You need to earn it.

Transparency

Building trust takes time, but the easiest way to achieve this is through consistent transparency. Transparency will strengthen your skills, promote better communication channels within the family and investments.

Transparency leads to better investment decisions and planning solutions. Transparency can improve your ability to solve problems and make better decisions. This is also key in maintaining high financial engagement.

By being open and honest, those around you can express their individual viewpoints instead of relying on a singular viewpoint. Your family/partner will want more transparency into decisions and more involvement in the decisions that affect them.

When your household is more engaged to work together to make the best decisions and achieve a common goal you experience the highest level of wealth creation.

Transparency is a secret to improving the financial experience. This experience not only makes you motivated, but also engaged in saving, investing, creative thinking processes for new strategies, and collaboration.

The day that you establish and embrace transparency you will begin to create a transparent culture that is good not just for you but also for the next generation for personal growth. This is where trust in you and from other people can come in.

People like seeing and hearing the truth. Just think about it, you are drawn to transparent individuals. You follow who you believe are transparent leaders. You stay loyal to transparent industries and products.

These days, being real and authentic can be challenging. But if you aim to succeed in your creation of wealth, you need to connect to people on a trust level and embrace true transparency.

It's a tool to help you stay on top of everything, placing special emphasis on your finances, and personal goals. My goal is to help you build a habit of success every day.

Financial transparency creates clear lines of communication and helps stamp out fear and uncertainty. Not only that, understanding the stories behind your wealth creation goals and arms our team with the information they need to make smart investment decisions.

Financial language is often unfamiliar and confusing, making even the simplest concepts seem complex. The first step to growing a financially literate household is making sure you're all speaking the same language.

When you sit down to discuss your budget and investment goals, did your family really understand? How about when you mentioned that defensive investments are needed? Beyond just vocabulary, does your family or even you have a clear understanding of how your day-to-day spending impacts the numbers?

Transparency

Financial transparency is the practice of sharing financial information across the household. At its full potential, it prompts a transformative shift in culture, equipping every member of the family with the knowledge and tools to participate in the household financials and savings and investing.

The goal is to be an open-book for money management and finances to give family members the knowledge and tools to help them understand how the household is run and what their stake is in the financial outcomes.

I promise when your family members understand this process, they're better able to adapt to changes, stay committed to your goals, and take ownership of their actions on a daily basis.

It all ties back to living out your core values and connecting everyone to your purpose. You must want everyone to have a meaningful answer when they are asked, "How's your wealth creation doing?"

Open-book money management deepens everyone's engagement by helping them understand how they can impact the future in their individual roles.

Being authentic and transparent creates the most successful environments that directly influence wealth creation. A culture defined by accountability, trust, and purposeful growth will have a loyal, engaged strategy.

This is why you must embrace financial transparency to strengthen the culture and improve wealth creation. TRUST!

Being financially transparent turns traditional, blind financials on its head by inviting family members to think like owners and innovate from the bottom up.

I recall having my clients read "What would the Rockefellers do?" It laid a foundation that this is about wealth creation, no, more about generational wealth creation.

So, let me be transparent about the foundation for generational wealth from the core. As a wealth creator you must be purpose-driven caring for the totality of the lives in your household, and financial transparency is a direct investment in the overall well-being of everyone.

You are doing this because sharing financials requires financial education. You have to equip them with valuable new skills that they can put to use in their personal lives to advance their saving and investing.

Best of all, financial education doesn't require employees to enroll in night school or read confusing textbooks — they'll increase their financial literacy by learning alongside coworkers and participating in the real-time realities of your company finances.

Transparency

The foundation is about having a complete financial discussion about the many financial behaviors you have learned are often based on how you grew up and the examples your parents set for you.

This series of Wealth Creation books is designed to counter any and all negative money practices and behaviors.

Be mindful not to pass judgment as you learn your household financial background. Understanding your partner's financial background can help you better understand their decision-making and vice versa.

Each of you should identify your individual financial goals and the steps or actions needed to achieve them. With that in mind, you and your household can then discuss how to integrate these goals into a set of common or shared goals.

No matter what your financial situation or goals entail, use these financial discussions as a chance to plan for the future. If you're not sure how to start a financial conversation, start with honesty! Approach your financial discussion at a time when you and your household are comfortable and relaxed.

When it comes to having difficult conversations, timing is everything. Even if you're embarrassed about your financial situation or debt accumulation, remaining honest with your household is certainly the best policy.

Finally, the term "generational wealth" implies an infinite security for your family for decades to come. Some assumptions about immense inheritance and family legacy, however, may not be true.

How long this wealth lasts, and how it's managed differs from generation to generation and doesn't always ensure a carefree, wealthy lifestyle.

Even with smart investments and money management skills they are not always passed down with wealth. A staggering number of wealthy families lose their wealth by the next generation, with even a larger number losing it the generation after that.

Sustaining substantial wealth takes financial savvy and transparency –something that not all wealthy parents are passing along to their heirs. It's reported that 64 percent of parents admit they've talked little very little (or not at all) about their wealth to their children.

Without that education, and with money going to several different children, the inheritance may be spent quickly without any means of recovery.

What's really coming through with transparency is truth. And truth always brings more truth. You'll likely become more truthful with yourself, and others are more likely to share their truth with you. Truth puts people at ease, and it's when we're at ease that our real brilliance can shine.

Transparency

It all starts with you. You cannot control how other people choose to be, but you can exercise your own influence. You can take 100% responsibility for how you choose to show up, for stepping into integrity, and for embracing transparency as the wealth creator.

I believe that you can change this, understanding every child of wealth needs to be given a roadmap of how to maintain and grow wealth. You can establish a daily briefing on the family's net worth, how your business runs, this doesn't simply happen because of bloodline.

Together you and I are breaking that cycle, and giving the next generation a plan of action with directions on how to spend, save, give back in philanthropic efforts and build sustainable wealth. TRUST

Chapter Six

Commitment

Your trust is given and earned inside of your commitment to yourself as well as the commitment of others. It is my opinion that trust is highly established when others see and experience you keeping your commitment.

What I hope for you in this chapter is to first review all of your plans, all of the goals that you have set for yourself, all of the new products and investments you are considering.

Not just to look at as a vision board, all of these choices you have made for yourself are now your financial and personal commitment.

Before I go deep into it I would like to share (be transparent) with you. When I was a young man growing up I was constantly in and out of trouble. So, I decided to go into the army, I remember deciding that this is what I wanted for myself.

I find myself getting on that greyhound bus in the middle of a cold Wednesday afternoon heading to Raleigh NC to catch Amtrak heading to Ft Jackson SC. This night time ride on the train was just like in the movies, I am seeing flashing lights and then complete darkness. So excited still.

Then we arrived, at the station there was this army cattle truck (Google it) outside, at the time I had never seen one before. Everyone was so nice upon arrival, we ate and waited for the next group of young men to arrive.

After an hour or so we politely start sharing experiences with being in a band or on a drill team. For me that was an awesome moment, yes I have been on a drill team, I was also the team leader. The drill sergeant was such a nice person, he called me and four other young men up and gave us our first promotion.

I was the platoon leader, the others were squad leader. So very happy at this point was I as we began to separate the men and place them into one of the four squads.

We load up on the army cattle truck and quietly travel to the base. The squad leaders and myself got off the truck with the drill sergeant and were met back by three other sergeants that changed the tide.

Horns went off, very loud horns blowing, with each of the sergeants now screaming at the top of their voice "get in your squad, get in your squad, move, move," it caused so much confusion that these young men began to cry, fall down and stumble over each other.

Man, what confusion and disorder was taking place.

I can assure you that none of us had ever seen anything like this before, nothing! This was my first realization that this was a commitment, whether I like it or not. I made this commitment, I signed the papers.

Weeks into this man's army I also realized that I didn't want to lead men. One morning we went on a 10 mile run, I wasn't feeling it on this day. Unlike other mornings I was not going to lead 128 men in a 10 mile run.

My drill sergeant was so angry at me, he pulled me to the side and began to let me have it about how my men will follow me, how excellent I must be at all times. He explained how this could be the first of many leadership roles in my life.

This is a commitment, other people's lives depend on it. I didn't care, I wanted out. As I got out over time there was something that he said to me that happened to challenge me outside of his command. He said; "Wilson, until you complete what you start, you will always be a quitter, the world may never know, but you will always know that you are a quitter. Life is about commitments".

Your future will depend on you not being a quitter, never giving up, your financial future likewise will be based on your commitment, and your relationship future will be based on your trustworthiness by you keeping your commitment.

I shared this story with you for the first time, I believe it is relevant because your next challenge is to stay committed to those things that you have determined is necessary for your wealth creation journey.

Let's get going here, your financial commitment is a commitment to all of the goals, strategies, investment plans, saving and asset accumulation for your future. You may use the term for either a major expense or an ordinary one.

Depending on your situation, the term may refer to either a very-long-term commitment or a one-off situation. Financial commitments exist in both your now and future world.

Even if your investment has not yet occurred, it's like you are entering into a financial commitment as a pledge to invest something on a future date or over a specific period. Some financial commitments may have an expiration date. Others, however, are ongoing and have no specific termination date.

Your Commitment

You also have a financial commitment. Yours is to pay back the money that you have borrowed. Specifically, your commitment is to pay back according to the specifications in the contract that you signed.

The debt and liability always seem to take the front seat whenever you talk about financial obligations. Notice the play on words here "obligations" are commitments that you made, but I want you to see them as obligations, this is important. I want you to move to another level by trusting yourself in this new space.

It is going to be your level of commitment to wealth creation that is going to decide your level of success in it. Sadly, most people just stop after they wish they were out of debt, only to create more debt. I guess that is a great time to say it, you are already a creator, a creator of debt and liabilities over and over.

There is also this space where you could choose to be a person who wishes and yearns. It is that 'wish' part and hardly takes on the pain to commit to their dreams. Probably that is what stops them from being successful in any endeavor.

Let's get this straight that there is no shortcut to success. The only way to be successful is to take the long road and follow your pursuit with one hundred percent dedication and commitment to it.

However, I want to be clear about the road to success. It isn't as easy as it may sound. You have to make several commitments to yourself to reach there and live the life you've dreamt in your dreams. Trust is a part of it all.

I can say this until my face changes colors. You have got to believe in yourself before others will start believing in you.

Whatever is that you would like to achieve, make sure that you believe in it and trust your abilities to accomplish it.

The main problem with you is that you tend to underestimate your capabilities that stop you from reaching your true potential.

You know this already: take a notebook and write your strengths, uniqueness, greatest achievements and accomplishments in it and read them aloud every morning. This little technique can do wonders to strengthen your belief in yourself and trust yourself.

I see so many clients with a lot of potential but their low self-esteem and lack of confidence is getting in their own way to success. I do not want this for you, so, it's essential to accept yourself and believe in abilities to live your best life. Every day!

Now that you know what you want to pursue in life, it's time to make an action plan for it. Whether your goals are small or big, you need to be committing yourself to take massive action every single day without any excuses. None!

It starts with you preparing your brain to passionately chase your dreams or whatever you are passionate about in life. You can begin by making a plan.

Well, there are many planning tools out there to help you out. While making your action plan, make sure you customize it as per your needs and strengths.

Don't be too casual or overly ambitious about them. Be as realistic as possible so that you are inspired enough to take massive action on them every day without any excuses.

Your Commitment

You being adaptable and learning continually will set you apart from those who would like to criticize you. Your adaptability and zeal to grow can take you places in life.

It's sad to see that people are so rigid in their thoughts and beliefs that they reject any suggestions or new approach given to them.

It can be dangerous for their career and overall life in general. It is not the strongest of the species that survives, or the most intelligent that survives. It is the one that is the most adaptable to change."

I want you to earn as much as you can from whoever you want as it would be something no one can take away from you. Never stop learning as most times there are more than one way to do the same thing.

The moment you shed your preconceived notions and embrace adaptability, opportunities will automatically present themself in the most unexpected ways.

You must be willing to have the willingness to lose some sleep, some friends and saying NO. Success often comes to those who are willing to do whatever it takes to be successful.

You would not only have to work your butt off but might have to say no to several things that don't align with your goals. But trust the commitment that you are making.

It might be tempting to go shopping or party with friends on weekends but working on your startup or wealth creation is what is going to take to make an actual difference. If you are working on your job during the day then the only way to work on your dream is by losing some sleep.

One more thing, start saying NO more often. It might take a lot of courage to say no to friends but doing it will make your life more successful and happier than theirs. There are two ways to succeed: the easy way and the difficult one.

Going for an easy way means doing 'whatever' it takes to reach there — by hook or by crook. It means taking shortcuts, favors, doing unethical things that go against the moral compass. Now, the commitment is not to do any of the things mentioned above.

You might get seduced with the idea of doing something unethical and get quick results. I will be talking much about getting quick results in the next book "The Speed".

However, for now – such things always come with a price — that can easily ruin everything within a snap of a finger. Remember that your journey to success is going to test your character along with dedication. Trust!

Do you know what the single most important thing in your life is? It's nothing else but your health. Your physical and mental health plays an important part in your life as everything directly or indirectly depends on it.

The reason I continue to incorporate the physical and mental into this wealth creation journey is because I need you to be complete.

So don't get too consumed in working hard that you start ignoring your health. If you've worked tirelessly for straight 40 hours, it makes sense to give your body the rest it deserves.

If you're working on weekends, try spending at least a few hours with your near and dear ones and recharge your physical and mental batteries.

Your Commitment

Always build your trust and never give up. No matter how cliché it may sound, the key to success is to never give up on yourself. As you walk through this process of wealth creation, you will fall down many times.

You might also make mistakes and fail, and it's absolutely okay. That is the part that most people never see of you, your commitment to stay and put in the hard work. As in everyone's life things will happen but never let anything hamper your wealth creation.

Keep in mind that in order to succeed and become your best version, you have to have a lot of faith in yourself. This indomitable spirit will help you get through these tough times a bit easily. Don't give up ever — come what may.

The thing about commitment is that it means staying loyal to what you said you were going to do long after the mood you said it in has left you. Now, it is up to you to commit yourself and act on things or let them happen.

My wrap up on commitment is really about you keeping your word to the things that you say you will do, it is your integrity, it is your character. Trust yourself by doing it with your entire being. Going through the motions doesn't count.

If you're going to do it, do it with your entire being. Show up fully. Put your whole heart into it. Or don't do it at all. Only half showing up for other people is painful to them. The same with only half showing up for yourself.

Remember your deeper Why. You're probably not taking your commitments seriously because you have forgotten why it's so important. It's just another thing on your endless to-do list.

Instead, remember the deeper reason you committed to this — maybe it's to create generational wealth.

Keep wealth creation in your heart, and make this commitment the most important thing in the world, at least at the moment you're doing it. Write out why you care so much about this commitment, and put that somewhere you can't miss it. Yes that again!

If you aren't fully doing it, ask what's holding you back. Notice if you're not really upholding your commitment, or if you're only going through the motions.

What's stopping you from fully showing up?
What's getting in the way?

There might be fear even at this stage, or maybe you aren't giving it enough weight and giving it the focus it deserves. Pause and be with this resistance or floppiness, and ask yourself what it would take to deepen this commitment.

Get out of commitments you are not going to uphold. You do not want to be overcommitted — which means you can't possibly meet all of your commitments.

In this case, you should first see if there's a way you can meet some of those commitments for as long as you said you would (work on saving and investing for a month in stocks, for example), but then get out of stocks once you have fulfilled that commitment. That should be your first choice — do what you said you would, but then end it when you can.

Next choice is to renegotiate the commitment if necessary — maybe you said you could do it for a year, but you can only do it for the next few months. Maybe you said you could do it every day, but all you are able to do is three days a week.

Lastly, get out of the commitment if you can't do either of the above. Again, recognize that this is necessary if you're going to fully meet your more important commitments.

So this is a matter of prioritizing which ones you need to meet. But if you have to get out of a commitment, let that be a grave lesson in overcommitting yourself. You have to trust you!

Chapter Seven

Consistency

The strength of trust as it relates to wealth creation seems to mirror my book "The Focus" and building a foundation on many of the same principles.

If you think about it, I mean honestly think about it you will understand that trust is the basis for every financial exchange and all endeavors.

Put very simple, when you trust you simply believe that the person or entity you are dealing with has the ability to meet the commitment—to provide you the resources you desire and actually need.

In short, honesty—or integrity—is your sense that promises well be kept and that person is not telling lies about the resources.

I learned a long time ago whenever any two people talk about trust they may think they're talking about the same thing when they actually aren't.

Yet, most people are not always aware of this ambiguity—or of the importance of trying to resolve it. It is almost completely unimportant to them.

It balls down to you trying to build trust by your intuition— in everyday life. Recognizing that building trust only by intuition set you up to never realize that maybe just maybe there are opportunities being missed in leveraging trust more effectively— with others.

Trust, after all, is a powerful force: it can win and even deepen new and important relationships on your journey. Relationships that you can't afford to rely on intuition alone for how you manage this trust.

With The Wealth Creation Series I am creating a unique body of knowledge by connecting readers like you from diverse backgrounds and sharing my ideas, concepts, and actionable insights in a series books that taking a systematic approach to the process of building trust in a financial environment that once closed its doors to you.

Now you have to come into this environment with consistency. I am talking about the kind of consistency with your views, ideals, and desires that you maintain despite all challenges from without. Trusting your ability to remain focused and steadfast to a process achieve result doing the thing right over time over and over again.

Wealth creation as you know by now (I am assuming that you have read the series books leading to this one) is a systematic process consistently do the same or similar thing over and over.

You have to stay consistent in wealth creation despite difficulty or delays in achieving success. You must have the ability to rapidly recover emotional and mental stability after a traumatic situation or even a victorious event.

I am so tired of people and organization always asking the question what is it that separates the wealthy from the poor. They know already! Believe me, I am talking about trust, there is so much out there talking about what it takes to become wealthy.

Trust this from me, what separates wealthy people from poor people is their consistency in taking action, even when they don't feel motivated. Being consistent is more important than being motivated, especially for long-term goals.

Do you realize that motivation is a passing feeling? It comes and goes, and it's not always easy to rely on much like intuition. On the other hand, consistency is a habit that you can cultivate over time. You can depend on it, even when you are not feeling motivated. This is important because consistency will help you achieve your goals in the long run.

Anyone who has ever tried to achieve a demanding goal knows that consistency is critical. Whether it's working out, eating healthy, or studying for an exam, there is no substitute for consistency when it comes to reaching your goals.

The reason is simple: consistency leads to momentum. The very moment that you begin to save as little as $19.76 a week you being to realize is simple or create an invest portfolio and buying shares of stocks over and over.

Habits

The more consistently you do something, the easier it becomes, and the more momentum you build up. You as a wealth creator must trust the process and be consistent.

Eventually, the very thing that was once a struggle becomes a habit, and habits are hard to break.

This is why consistency is so important- it is the key to making lasting change. So if you're looking to achieve a goal, remember to be consistent (no matter what), and eventually, you'll reach your destination.

Set realistic goals around the things that you trust. In my next book "The Speed" I will introduce you to products and provide you speed to wealth creation. This will mean that you will need trust to accomplish all of your goals.

With the exception of trust your goals must be realistic; otherwise, you are setting yourself up for failure. You are more likely to give up when you set unrealistic goals because you can't seem to achieve them.

You also here all of the time to get an accountability partner, you will need a partner that you can trust. If you can trust someone to hold you accountable it will be a great way to stay on track. When you know someone depends on you, you are more likely to follow through.

I may get in trouble with this one. I do not want you to see your accountability partner as simple as a study buddy or some workout partner. This is your financial life that you building, it's not simple this for generations. Having that role model: It's helpful to have someone you can look up to who is consistent in their actions. This will help you stay consistent and on track when you feeling down.

Another thing that I believe will aid you in your area of trust is to set a schedule. Having a set schedule and deadlines will help you be more consistent because it gives us structure.

When you know when you need to do something, it's easier to follow through and having a deadline to meet, you are more likely to be consistent in our actions. You don't want to let yourself down, and you want to finish the task at hand.

It becomes a habit that you trust and the speed of everything behind trust and habit is one of the best ways stay consistent by turn your goal into a habit and lifestyles. Once something becomes a habit, you do not even have to think about it- it's just something you do.

Don't underestimate the power of a routine! Your new routines will be helping you to be more consistent because it becomes second nature. You know what you need to do and when, so there's less room for error.

You are securing yourself by not trying to do too much at once. That can be overwhelming, and it's often one of the reasons why people give up.

You will stick with it you should not trouble by starting small because it's not as daunting. You will always increase your goals over time, but it's essential to start small, so you don't get discouraged.

As a wealth creator you will be achieving more financial goals. Being consistent in your actions, you should know that you more likely to achieve all of your goals. This is because you putting in the effort on a daily basis, and you will not giving up halfway through.

This book on trust and the areas that I am talking about is to help you be more productive. Consistent saving, not just putting money in a jar or envelop, you have to be more intentional because you do not want to be wasting time on things that don't matter.

You know what you need to do and get it done without procrastinating. If you need too, go back and re-read "The Mindset" and/or "The Focus".

This is all about you being more reliable to the people who respect consistency because it's a sign they can trust. When you are consistent in our actions, people know they can count on you to do what you say you will do.

You are breaking generational curses by the consistent good habits you are developing by doing the same thing repeatedly until it becomes a part of who you are.

You trusting you show who you are in your actions living a life that aligns with your values and you are not constantly starting and stopping new things.

As I move forward, it may have sound like I took a shot at motivation or inspiration by pushing being consistent with building habits over feeling motivated. I meant every word that I said.

However, I have not made it this far in life without having some form of motivation and inspiration. I do not want you to get confused between motivation and inspiration. Motivation comes from within, whereas inspiration comes from external sources.

When you are motivated, you set a goal for yourselves and want to achieve it. But when you have inspiration, on the other hand, is when you see something that inspires you to take action.

You know exactly what it feels like to be motivated. That little voice inside your head tells you to keep going even when you feel like giving up. It gets you out of bed in the morning and helps you stay focused throughout the day.

And while motivation is important, it's not the only thing that drives you to achieve your goals. Inspiration is just as powerful, if not more so. Inspiration is what you will feel when you see someone else accomplishing something great.

It's what drives you to be better than you were yesterday. It's what fills you with hope and determination. So, next time you're feeling down, remember that motivation and inspiration are two of the most powerful forces in your world. Use them to your advantage, and you'll be unstoppable. Trust!

Habits

It's essential to be both motivated and inspired, but it's more important to be consistent. Yelp, I am back to it, motivation can come and go, but you will most likely take action if you inspired by something. This is why it's crucial to be surrounded by things that inspire you and seek out new sources of inspiration.

In order to be successful and have the wealth creation you desire, you need to have a combination of consistency and motivation. Motivation creates the crucial inertia required for consistency. It is my opinion that you learn to trust thing that you know to be consistent.

Don't worry – if you begin to feel like you cannot do this, please remember everyone has days when they don't feel motivated to work or even get out of bed - that's normal!

You will have days when you don't feel motivated. It's normal to feel this way from time to time. Maybe you are feeling stressed about dealing with a personal issue.

Whatever the reason, it's important to remember that these feelings are temporary. They will pass.

Take a break: Step away from whatever you're supposed to be doing. Take a walk, listen to music, or read a book. Give yourself some time to relax and rejuvenate.

Change your environment: Sometimes, all you need is a change of scenery. If you are working from home, try going to a coffee shop or the library. If you're stuck in a rut, changing your environment can help jump-start your creativity.

Talk to someone: When you are feeling down, it's helpful to talk to someone about it. This can help you process your feelings and develop a plan of action. Talking to a friend or family member can also help you feel supported.

Take action: Sometimes, the best way to get out of a 'rut' is to take action. Start working on that project you've been procrastinating on, or go for a walk around your neighborhood.

Even if it's small, doing something can help you get out of your rut.

Just make sure that you're more consistent than not, and eventually, you'll start to see the results you want. But make sure these days are kept to a minimum.

Maybe if you're feeling like that, especially if you've created a habit, you could be burnt out? Don't forget to take a break every once in a while! You need to recharge to continue wealth creation.

It may not be flashy, but it will yield substantial results over time. Consistency is like compound interest in that it builds over time. The more consistent you are, the more progress you will make. And this progress will eventually add up, resulting in significant changes in your live.

Anyone who has ever tried to establish a new routine knows that consistency is vital. It can be all too easy to start strong and then fizzle out a few weeks later.

But just like compound interest, consistency leads to results. The more consistent you are with your invest routine, the better results you will see. And those results will compound over time, leading to even more motivation to stick with it.

So you are focus and trusting your investment routine, remember that consistency is key. Just like compound interest, it will pay off in the long run.

We've already established that motivation alone is not a driver that can be thoroughly relied upon. However, don't underestimate the power of motivation - it still plays a crucial part!

Anyone who has ever achieved a goal knows the importance of motivation. It is the driving force that helps you keep going when things get tough, and it allows you to see the light at the end of the tunnel.

Without motivation, it would be all too easy to give up on your dreams and settle for a life of mediocrity.

Thankfully, motivation is something that you can cultivate. By setting yourself consistent goals and taking small steps towards them each day, you will gradually build up your motivation until it becomes an unstoppable force.

So whatever your goals may be, don't underestimate the power of motivation – it could be the key to making them a reality.

Finally, trust that consistency helps you find a system that works for you, meaning it will be easier to stick with. Be patient. It'll take time to see results. So don't get discouraged if you don't see immediate changes - consistency is key! Like they say, Rome was not built in a day!

OH! OH! OH! Let me just remind you how powerful this seemingly incredibly boring (consistency) thing is. It doesn't sound sexy, it lacks glamour and excitement at first sight, wait I might be lying. The end results can be very glamorous and exciting.

Because when you look at it more closely, consistency is anything but boring. It is the key to achievement and success. It is a magical power that can transform your life forever, for generations to come.

Consistency is the act of repeating the same action regularly and without exceptions. Saving – investing, saving – investing, accumulating assets, consistent action is the opposite of erratic behavior.

Consistency creates powerful habits; lack of consistency and exceptions mean that you have to start building the habits all over again.

Nearly any goal worth achieving demands regular and consistent efforts. It's the same whether you want to get a black belt in a martial art, master a musical instrument, or become an accomplished writer like me. You have to show up again and again, whether you feel like it or not.

Habits

There is a magic to consistency, from my experience in working with clients, those who take consistent action are the ones who achieve their goals. And you better know those who don't just dream of doing so.

Your daily efforts create your habits and habits make it easier to make those daily efforts. It's kind of like a feedback system that creates a snowball effect.

But to get that snowball effect takes hard work and determination. The effect is watching your money and assets grow.

Consistency doesn't just happen it requires planning.

What are your business goals?

What are your priorities?

What steps do you need to take to reach your goals?

What repetitive actions are required?

What needs to happen?

What needs to stop happening?

What do you have to let go of?

Are your priorities aligned with your core values?

TRUST!

Chapter Eight

The Principles

Your principles are built on the foundation of self-awareness. They are the "what" and "why" of what you do, and they often become the values of your wealth creation journey.

We talked about you having self-awareness earlier in this process in various ways. I want you to understand that without being self-aware, your principles will always be hard to find—and harder to commit to. Knowing what you stand for and why will guide your ability to wealth creation.

Listen carefully, you are on a journey as a wealth creator, how your mindset of being a creator of wealth must be different from the typical person trying to save money. In my experience, a wealth creator (YOU) mind is made up of five key layers to guide you as you trust yourself as a creator.

These five key layers involve your self-awareness, principles, prioritization, discipline and presence. The bible teaches that the Lord showers His Blessing on all, the just and the unjust.

You are like everyone around that has these five layers. However, you don't always devote enough energy to all of them.

The Principles

I would bet you that you are often obsessed with discipline and presence—arguably the shallowest layers—while completely neglecting the other, deep-level ones. Remember, working from the top down is like trying to build a house on sand.

As stated before in various ways self-awareness is your ability to act as an objective observer of your own behavior. Self-awareness should shape everything you do, and this is where toxic identities and belief systems live.

Here are a few examples, thoughts like "I'm shy," "I'm bad at technology" or "The hard way is the only way" are found in the self-awareness layer of the mindset too often.

As a wealth creator you will need to be able to take a bird's-eye view of your own thinking processes, recognize your strengths and weaknesses and create a new identity that helps you be the kind of person who accomplishes big things.

You gaining self-awareness starts with noticing how your minds work in the first place. A vital component of that is not beating yourself up for the negative or toxic habits you notice. Just notice them without judgment. To notice a pattern is to interrupt it, and that's the first step to change.

Trust and its principles is a powerful tool for building the kind of mindfulness you are going to need. When the goal is to focus on nothing but wealth creation and legacy, it's easy to notice what intrusive thoughts bubble up.

Maybe you begin free-writing in a journal to create another way to externalize your internal process. You can even deputize your friends or colleagues, asking them to point out negative self-talk that you didn't realize had become a habit. "Habit Police"

A significant proportion of your wealth creation will center on trust. Whether with banking or investing, people and critical issues all around trust the same. Without trust, the best anyone can hope for is average success.

The pandemic has created these lockdown conditions which have changed the mindset and the thinking space to bring the best of your abilities together into a new vision, the critical theme is centered on Trust.

Your world is changing, trust will be even more critical for your wealth creation. Without it, there will be little creativity, agility, challenge, nor happiness, no savings (maybe), certainly no wealth creation.

Having a focus on building trust is essential, another key principle of trust is that you focus on transparency, having an openness and accessibility of the wealth creation process, clear (rather than hidden) agendas and a determination to include all relevant family members rather than sideline just yourself.

You will have to make some tough decisions. By being transparent you will help those in your circle to understand the reasons behind those decisions and connect them with your direction and purpose.

The Principles

This implies that you make your direction clear and open, not with not-quite-true reasoning, or with no reasoning at all.

The people around you, or should I say the people that you build your new circle of influence with would want to see that you are relatable. When you are relatable, it means that other people can bond or associate with you because they perceive a "common ground."

Do not be surprised to discover that people may see you being relatable and get it confused with likability, but the two concepts are not the same. Being relatable is more about interacting with each person on an individual basis and showing that you connect with them.

It's the demonstration of empathy, showing that you care about others, understand their particular pressures and are ready to support their specific needs. Being relatable enables people to trust your heart (intentions).

Trust principles create predictability, when you are predictable, people "know what to expect" about your future behavior. This is not a lack of creativity; instead, it is stability and consistency. Predictability enables people to trust your actions.

The moment you begin to show your commitment to wealth creation, your action to the values that you have set will speak volume about your focus and feasibility.

You see, your feasibility is about your ability to evaluate a situation and create a coherent plan forward towards your wealth creation. Dreams can be inspiring, but that's all they will remain without a feasible plan of action. Trust Principles!

It's okay to dream-big and rally your circle around you and achieve huge ambition. However, if this is based more on hope, fuelled by personality rather than careful thought and a feasible plan of action, your circle will soon lose engagement and trust will fade. Your next big idea will fall flat without a second thought.

This may have happened to you already, nobody trusts you anymore. It is hard to bring others together and believe in you and your vision once the trust has faded. When I was growing I was a con artist, I never was up to any good. What those around me saw was nothing less than undesirable.

Today, regardless of my work with the U.S. Treasury, being an ambassador for the State of Georgia and a published author, there are people in my circle that just can't trust me.

Listen as the wealth creator you can build trust over time with intelligent, effective planning. When plans serve as a roadmap to the realization of dreams, your circle of friend become faithful advocates and believers. Your commitment to feasibility enables people to trust your judgment.

This journey of wealth creation is built up of many different processes, and those emerge from disciplines. Each of your disciplines might have several processes that branch out from it.

For example, the discipline of savings gives rise to the processes of loose change savings, weekly saving, dividend reinvestment, etc.

Do not get trapped believing there's a single, perfect process that will help you unlock untold riches. I want to say this as loud as I can, even if you master a process, you can get stuck right there because that's only one piece of your wealth creation puzzle.

Please do not ignore all of the foundational layers to focus on the thing that you know will get results fast. As you develop the trust mindset you will always know that the process is just a means to an end.

Yes, processes are how you will function, without mastering what you are learning in the series you may not generate the wealth you want.

Are you willing to risk making mistakes as long as those mistakes arise from reasonable thinking and effort?

Are you willing to invest resources into developing yourself and the people around continually, rather than expecting to just arrive one day?

It is said that you have to "start at the bottom" in order to make it. This is true! My Bishop Dale C. Bronner always teaches that "the only place you can start out on top is when you are digging a grave".

This is about you building the right mindset. Just take that first step toward self-awareness and you'll be well on your way!

What would help others trust you in ways that are life changing?

Are you a dedicated person who is a hard-worker?

Are you known to be on time? Are you known to keep your word?

These questions may not seem as much, but you have to realize that earning real trust will get you the reputation of being someone who's reliable and competent. When you say you'll do something, you actually do it.

You must begin creating emotional trust by going above and beyond what's expected of you, and creating meaningful bonds with your family and your circle of friends.

It requires a level of emotional intelligence. My experience has taught me that having high levels of emotional intelligence is definitely a good skill to start developing.

Wealthy people want people around them that they can trust. Likewise, you need to be a person that can be trusted. Have you ever had a best friend at work, then there's likely a lot of emotional trust between you. You knew that you had each other's backs. You treated each other with respect.

And you felt comfortable sharing ideas, thoughts, and feelings that you may not have expressed with others. Building

The Principles

trust in this way is more complex as it doesn't follow a set formula. It's more about networking and relationship building.

Your ability to create wealth will be impacted also by your emotional trust, learning how to build trust in the financial community is necessary if you want to create lasting relationships.

Having a high-trust environment gives opportunity that leads into more decision-making and information-sharing freedom. You want to create an environment where people feel comfortable sharing their thoughts and helping each other out.

To have a sense of well-being and good mental health, you need to know that other people understand you and have your best interests at heart.

This comes with having high levels of trust. It gives you peace of mind to know that everyone is working together.

I know that everyone is going to like you because of your wealth and as long as you have all of this wealth they will continue. However, it is likely that if you lose the wealth you may lose some folks around you.

Being trustworthy also makes you more likable. It makes you more likely to keep relationships and be a positive influence to others. It unlocks potential for new or faster growth with wealth creation. It's not just you that will do

Chapter Nine

The Bridge

There is so much for me to try and unwrap this final chapter of "The Trust". This is the book that I hope finalizes your commitment as a wealth creator. Just in case you didn't know, the first book of the series is "The Mindset".

"The Mindset" purpose is to open the door for you to see wealth creation as a possibility in your own life, it deals with you understanding you can make the decision to pursue wealth regardless of your current or past situation. It also lays a foundation for you to think and act differently.

The second book "The Influencer" helps you to identify things, situations, people, jobs, decisions and environments that impact the way you have dealt with wealth creation. What is really inside of you that is driving how you view wealth and those who have it.

"The Credit Score" this book may have upset a few people because of my approach. I want to be clear that credit is not the tool for wealth creation.

I know that there are many arguments that say differently, my personal quotes state, "Poor people daily check their credit score and wealthy people weekly review their net worth". Rob Wilson

The Bridge

"The Focus" is to bring you front and center to what it is you are about to do in your financial life. It is about you putting real meaning and effort to wealth creation. It is about your conversion to becoming a creator wealth, no longer watching and wanting to participate, you are the creator of wealth transfer.

Now, you are here, the final leg of the series, the book before "The Speed of Wealth Creation" is guiding you. "The Trust", right here, may be the biggest most important book of the series.

If you cannot trust the process, trust the commitment, trust yourself with money, trust those around you then you are reading for entertainment purposes and not as a wealth creator.

This would mean that there is absolutely no reason at all for you to want to read "The Speed", trust is the bridge that is going to allow you the ability to understand what is necessary for you to go to the next level of your financial growth. This chapter, I hope it to be the most powerful tool you will receive from the series.

Before I go any further I want to take this time to honor the senior pastor at the church I attended for the last twenty-two years. I have known Pastor Dale Bronner since he was a toddler,

I have served him breakfast, lunch and dinner many days of his life. I know of his character and his integrity and his love of God and his ability to be a shepherd.

I have for many years respected his teaching and have in fact taken lots of the insight and knowledge he has and have passed it onto others for their benefit. Recently, when I first cracked open the draft for "The Trust" I saw a quote from Pastor Dale on Facebook. The quote immediately resonated with me and I am making it a part of the message I want you to gain from the book.

I am going to try to incorporate his post into this final chapter on trust while delivering to you what I believe is needed on your journey. So, I really hope that I can give you more insight for your next chapter as a wealth creator.

This is his post as it was written:

Trust is an accelerator...
Trust is a bridge
Bridges are built to preserve time and energy
Bridges are built to make exchange possible
Bridges give access to synergistic opportunities and new possibilities
Distrust and suspicion are bridge burners...
Trust is a risk...so is distrust.

Pastor Dale Bronner Jr.
Senior Pastor Word of Faith Family Worship Cathedral

As he stated trust is an accelerator... I opened up this book talking about my relationship with Stephen Covey the author of "The Speed of Trust", everything about that book can be summed up in one word "Accelerator". This is where I will share my faith and trust in God.

The Bridge

This quote from Pastor Dale was purposeful and done in a divine manner and timing. When trust is present everything is on the move, it acts as the fuel that drives you to your destination much sooner than without trust. Your ability to accumulate wealth is greatly impacted by trust.

Trusting in yourself and others will be tested. As I talk about trust I want to relate it to a bridge, I am going to incorporate the elements of a bridge to establish it as a financial action to help you to continue to have an open mind.

When you see trust as a bridge you know that it is a structure carrying a pathway or roadway over an obstacle (like a river), when I speak of a "financial bridge" I want you know it is about the techniques when setting goals, the wealth creation goals that will drastically improve and enhance your chances of accomplishing those goals.

If trust changes the speed of everything then you understand how bridges are designed to speed up as well, it preserves time and energy. When you trust someone or something during business or any other engagement it makes every exchange a possibility.

Trust opens the door for you to have access to synergistic opportunities and new possibilities as you cross over into a different circle of friends and relationships.

When trust is not present there are a lot of reasons why you might want to delay your next strategic planning process. You should know by now operating without a trust will slow your momentum towards your long-term goals.

If you look at trust as a bridge that gets you across financial challenges, debt and liabilities and now it will connect you to wealth accumulation and creation. You understand that this type of trust between people is like a bridge.

However, it must be built from both sides of your journey. When it is built with care and careful planning, it will be durable — capable of weathering the storms of life.

The importance of trust at this level is vital for you. Your relationship with bankers, brokers and advisors will need to be built from both sides with the intent of you staying on course as a wealth creator. Establishing your trust (financial target) plan so that it will be able to allow you to be successful and guide you.

Occasionally, you will need reassurances and required commitment maintenance; when you have a solid built trust you will feel safe putting a great deal of your emotional weight on the bridge — it's where keeping one's promises is expected; sensitive secrets divulged are carefully protected; and personal flaws, weaknesses are accepted and wealth creation flows.

Building the bridge called trust can be and in many ways costly, risky, and requires a substantial time investment, but the rewards are truly fulfilling. Happy are those who have one or two close relationships! Happy are those who create multiple sources of wealth creation.

The Bridge

There will be a time that trust, maybe a large section of that trust bridge is washed away through betrayal, deception, or broken promises. The ache and bitterness can be almost unbearable. The wonderful benefits that spring from trusting relationships are worth the risk of potential heartache.

Know there are no quick fixes for the pain caused, nor any shortcuts to getting back to the way things were. A great deal of patience and humility is needed to hear the other's pain. Accept responsibility for your actions without blaming others or explaining them away.

Accept the consequences of your actions, including the emotional distance, and make restitution when possible. Be accountable for your actions without becoming defensive.

The trust bridge must be rebuilt from both sides.

Is it possible to rebuild the trust bridge?
How can you be sure it won't be washed out again?

Think of it this way,

Your trust bridge (financial target) plan is a short-term strategic plan that "bridges" the gap between strategic plan cycles. You should want your strategic plan to cover a 3–5 year horizon and take 6–12 months to create – a bridge (financial target) plan only covers a 1–2 year horizon and takes about 3–5 months to create.

Often, a bridge of trust (financial target) plan is best designed as an extension of the existing plan. It is more streamlined and focused than a regular strategic plan and focuses more on tactics aligned with an existing strategic focus. Now more than ever your saving and investing is critical!

A bridge of trust (financial target) plan allows you to continue to pursue defined strategic pathways during times of uncertainty or rapid, unpredictable change. It's also a good solution for when you are overwhelmed due to a highly volatile, uncertain, complex and confusing financial market.

If you're dealing with a personal burnout and overwhelm, a bridge of trust (financial target) plan allows you to take a breath before launching into a deliberate, time-consuming planning process. You may get tired; pursuing a trust bridge (financial target) plan gives you a moment of grace.

When might it make sense to do a bridge plan? There are many different reasons you might pursue a bridge (financial target) plan before you do your next strategic plan.

You should allow time for wealth creation to keep positive momentum going while you are charting a pathway forward focused on promoting wealth creation success, equity, and institutional thriving.

How do we get started with a bridge plan?

The Bridge

Weigh the pros and cons of moving forward with a short-term bridge plan. Does it make sense to continue the pursuit of existing strategic pathways? Or do you need to create an integrated strategic plan that outlines a future-focused wealth creation strategy?

Determine if your plan for wealth creation possesses the necessary human capital and financial resources to commit to a deliberate strategic planning process that may take up to 16 to 24 months.

Identify what your goals are in designing a bridge (financial target) plan. In particular, how could it help you reach stability in the face of a volatile marketplace?

I don't mean to be getting fancy here, but what needs to be considered about rebuilding your trust bridge is that you should place a name to this bridge. A financial bridge isn't as fancy as it sounds. It's actually something that is relatively simple.

There will be other bridges in your life that are the result of trust, like the financial bridge that you are about to learn, there is a relationship bridge, a work environment bridge, a family bridge and a community bridge. There will always be bridges to create action plans to build and strengthen as you have growth.

Creating your financial bridge would force you to create action items. When you create the financial bridge for your goals you would list out all the actions you plan on taking.

Not just say you have an action plan. People know they need a budget, people know they need a plan, most of them will tell you that they have one. Do make that mistake!

You know the importance of transportation. You use different modes of transportation for different purposes. Transportation is selected according to your needs like distance to be covered, the time you have, money you have to spend.

These various forms of transportation are horseback, buggy, bikes, public, car, bus, train, plane and sea are available to all.

Each of them has a different class, a different level, a different standard, a different comfort and mode of appreciation. Your action plans for your financial bridge has to be one of appreciation and comfort for you.

Consider this as you seek to create a new standard for you, remember that where transportation is lacking, disadvantages are prominent for those who need access to transit services to access opportunities. The same is true is wealth creation, generational wealth transfer. Trust, what about trust, and do not fall into the mode of just surviving.

Create your to do is list out the specific drivers of the wealth creation you want to have and create a visual "bridge". A visual bridge very similar to a vision board, in fact I have a plan and have done much of the work for you. When you look at page 118 in "The Mindset", there you will find many of the components you will need and your strategy.

The Bridge

Just do not rely on my list, create your own list for your comfort and to help reach your goal. You must list out where you are forecasting your increase to come from, but also listing out how that increase will become a reality.

Keep in mind that this is an extremely simplified example. Creating a financial portfolio can get much more complex when you are forecasting for generational wealth. Typically there will be revenue, expense, taxes, and dividends for each line item to consider.

Trusting and using the "Financial Portfolio" technique when setting goals will be a great benefit to your future. In fact, you can use the financial bridge technique for goals that are both financial and non-financial in nature.

It doesn't have to be just for wealth creation. It can really be used to lay out an actionable plan for any personal goals you might have.

Let me show another example to give you a better idea of how this could work for a non-financial goal. Let's say you want to gain 3 new technology stocks within the next two months.

What actions do you have to take that realistically will result in gaining 3 new stocks?

In reality you would want to write out exactly when you plan on purchasing these items, which will become an action step.

There is also a risk that each action step does not result in new stocks but the purchase of more currently owned stocks. On the flip side, there are opportunities built in because there is a chance that you may gain more stocks than first thought.

One reason using the financial portfolio technique is useful is because people like to talk about goals but not on how they plan on achieving them.

A financial portfolio forces you to visualize how you will achieve your goals. It also forces you to think about whether or not your assumptions are realistic.

If a goal seems like it will be easier than expected to accomplish it may be time to think about a "stretch" goal, in other words something that will be difficult to achieve but still realistic.

What are your thoughts on using the "Financial Portfolio" technique to accomplish goals? How do you hold yourself accountable to your goals? Accountability is a powerful thing. For every goal there have to be concrete action steps in place. Otherwise it's just a wish.

In my last book of the series "The Speed" I hope to give you the complete model of building your financial portfolio. You will need to trust yourself in creating new consistency action steps regardless of how small they seem right now.

The Bridge

Recently, I heard something that really made me realize how important your decision in wealth creation really is.

Twenty year from now you are going to wish that you have the health and knowledge that you have right now. You are going to want the same vision, the same strength, the same memory, the same taste for food and the same opportunities.

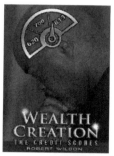

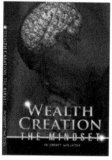